v//~ new

DATE DUE   3/02

MAY 29 05			
FEB 1 4 2004			
GAYLORD			PRINTED IN U.S.A.

SUNFLOWERS

SUNFLOWERS

LINDSAY PORTER

PHOTOGRAPHS BY DEBBIE PATTERSON

LORENZ BOOKS

NEW YORK • LONDON • SYDNEY • BATH

Picture Credits
The publishers would like to thank Christies Images for the photograph on page 8 (top),
e t archive for the photographs on page 8 (bottom), 10 and 11 (bottom) and the
Bridgeman Art Library for the photographs on pages 9 and 11 (top).

This edition published in 1996 by Lorenz Books
an imprint of Anness Publishing Limited
administrative office: 27 West 20th Street
New York, NY 10011

Lorenz Books are available for bulk purchase for sales promotion and for premium use.
For details write or call the manager of special sales, LORENZ BOOKS, 27 West 20th Street,
New York, NY 10011; (212) 807-6739.

ISBN 1 85967 144 6

Publisher: Joanna Lorenz
Assistant Editor: Sarah Ainley
Copy Editor: Deborah Savage
Designer: Lilian Lindblom
Step Photographer: Lucy Tizard
Illustrator: Lucinda Ganderton
Introduction by Tessa Evelegh

Printed in Singapore by
Star Standard Industries Pte Ltd

Contents

INTRODUCTION

Sunflowers! Van Gogh knew all about the exuberance of sunflowers. His famous painting of them jostling for space in a pot-bellied vase has proved to be a favorite among all ages for many generations. Its appeal must be the sheer audacity of the loud, bright blooms that can't help but lift the spirits of anyone who sets eyes on them. Perhaps it is the simplicity of sunflowers that wins our affections. Certainly, they are popular among children who invariably put them at the top of their list of favorite flowers to grow, and very often, to draw too. Or perhaps, it's their sheer size that we admire. For we all know that they can grow to a relatively dainty two foot height, but if we're being honest, it's the giant twelve footers with their generous 1 ft blooms that capture our imagination. However, in the Victorian language of flowers, dwarf sunflowers indicate adoration, while the tall ones mean haughtiness. So if we were to give sunflowers as a gift to anyone familiar with flower meanings, we would probably favor the smaller.

Sunflower is a literal translation of the botanical name of this audacious bloom, being *Helianthus* – *helios* (the sun) and *anthos* (flower) – though it is thought that this is because of its habit of turning to the sun throughout the day, rather than its sun-like appearance. However, its size and the generous bright petals are symbolic of the sun itself, and images of sunflowers evoke a warm summer's day, even in the dead of winter. The sunflower's appearance has appealed to people down the centuries who have used it as a motif on all manner of artifacts. In their native Peru, the Aztecs wrought sunflowers in pure gold to decorate their Temples of the Sun and for their priestesses to wear as jewelery. The priestesses also wore sunflowers

Above: Lalique gold and enamel brooch decorated with sunflowers.

on their heads and carried them during religious ceremonies. Magnificent golden sunflowers also caught the imagination of the conquering Spaniards who brought them to Europe in the early 16th century. They soon became established as a mainstay of typical cottage gardens, and from an economic point of view, it was discovered that every part of this fast-growing giant could be put to use. The leaves were used as cattle food, the petals for dye, the stems for making paper, and, most important, the seeds could be pressed for a high quality cooking oil.

It was in Russia that the sunflower took on greatest significance, becoming a valuable source for food, animal fodder and oil. Its introduction by Peter the Great toward the end of the 16th century was lucky since it came after the Russian Orthodox Church had published its list of prohibited oil-rich foods to be avoided in Lent.

Left: Botanical study of sunflowers by J Miller.

As a motif, the sunflower is a gift for anyone wanting to add brightness and decoration to any craft, since its simple form is easy to recreate. At its simplest, a sunflower can be a large, dark circle ringed by orange petals, which is easy enough even for a young

Left: Silk with sunflower motif by Maison Ogier & Duplan, Lyon, 1894.

Below: Sunflowers by Vincent Van Gogh, 1888.

So sunflowers took on great importance, providing both oil and seeds, which were roasted and eaten whole. This led to the development of the Russian Sunflower, the king of all sunflowers which became known as the Mammoth or Giant Sunflower, so-called because the heads reach a staggering 15 in across, each containing 2,000 seeds.

Mammoth or not, as well as having a sunlike appearance, this bountiful plant also seemed almost to mimic the sun itself in its life-enhancing qualities. Soon, this beneficial, flamboyant flower became adopted as a favorite motif, being used to decorate furniture, sundials, ceramics and tiles. It also made appearances in intricate needlework since embroiderers down the ages were inspired by the rich, golden colors.

child to manage. You can paint them on boxes, walls of children's rooms, ceramics or papier-mâché artifacts. Groups of sunflowers can look wonderful, too. For variation, paint some with larger middles and smaller petals or the opposite way. The basic sunflower form also provides a perfect motif for crafts because its clear outline is easy to cut out in many media. Use it as inspiration for appliqué designs, potato and lino cuts, mosaics and relief papier-mâché work, all of which rely on uncomplicated forms to be effective. It can be wonderful for collage and embroidery work, too, since the massed seeds can be easily recreated with any kind of material. Try peppercorns for collage; tiny black beads

or French knots for embroidery. Sunflowers can be sophisticated, too. In the hands of an artist, subtle color variations can be given to their softly ridged petals; great texture to their generous seeded middles. Take inspiration from Van Gogh's post-Impressionist style in his famous Sunflowers painting, lending texture with browns, tans and oranges.

As well as the obvious orange-yellow tones, you can use metals in brass, bronze and gold effects for petals. For appliqué and embroidery, try metallic threads and fabrics for a rich, burnished look. For backgrounds to sunflowers, take inspiration from sunny climes where the flowers are often grown *en masse*. Think French fields in summertime, when the skies are the color of azure and

Left: La Torre Art Nouveau bedside table, 1907–10.

*Left: Sunflowers by
Paul Gauguin, 1901.·*

*Below: Detail from a cover for
an arts magazine by Eugene
Grasset, c. 1895.*

turquoise, setting off the serried ranks of merry blooms. Or go for a strong, vibrant look by setting them against scarlet, orange or even deep purple. These are just nuggets of inspiration. The pages of this book bring color and form to that inspiration with a variety of tempting projects for you to make for yourself, using a wide range of materials. Recreate the gifts from the pages or adapt what you see, substituting alternative materials, or altering shapes to bring your own flair and creativity to a truly original piece.

PAPIER-MACHE PITCHER WITH SUNFLOWER

This pitcher looks like a modern Italian ceramic, with its elegant shape and brilliant colors, but in fact, it's made from papier-mâché shaped around a blown-up balloon. A sunflower molded from paper pulp makes a relief decoration.

YOU WILL NEED

MATERIALS
balloon
newspapers
wallpaper paste
thin cardboard
round margarine container
masking tape
fine string
acrylic paints: blue, yellow, red and green
clear varnish

FOR THE PAPIER-MACHE PULP
5 sheets newspaper
5 teaspoons white glue
2 teaspoons wallpaper paste
1 teaspoon plaster of Paris
1 teaspoon linseed oil

EQUIPMENT
scissors
paint-mixing container
medium and fine paintbrushes

1 Blow up the balloon, and tie a knot in the end. Tear thin strips of newspaper. Soak in the wallpaper paste, and cover the balloon with at least eight layers of papier-mâché. Allow to dry thoroughly. Cut slits in the top of the balloon at the knot end, and remove the balloon. Cut out a V-shape in one side. Cut a piece of cardboard to form a spout. Tape it in position.

TO MAKE THE PAPIER-MACHE PULP
Tear the paper into pieces about 1 in square, and put them in an old saucepan with water to cover. Simmer for about half an hour. Spoon the paper and any water into a blender, and purée it. Pour into a suitable lidded container. Add the white glue, wallpaper paste, plaster of Paris and linseed oil. Stir vigorously. The pulp is now ready to use.

2 Cut off the rim of an old margarine container for the base. Bind it to the bottom with masking tape. To make the handle, roll up some glued newspaper sheets, and curve the roll to fit the pitcher. Allow to dry thoroughly. Then cover the handle with string, leaving about ½–1 in uncovered at each end. Cut two slits in the side, and insert the handle.

3 Model the pulp on the side of the pitcher in the shape of sunflowers and leaves. Allow to dry overnight. Paint the background, flowers and details. Allow to dry. Finally, give the whole pitcher a coat of varnish.

GOLD-RIMMED SUNFLOWER BOWL

This attractive bowl is delicately hand painted and decorated with gold paint. Its cheerful, sunny design will brighten up any dull corner. Use it purely as decoration or to hold trinkets, nuts or sweets.

YOU WILL NEED

MATERIALS
petroleum jelly
newspaper
papier-mâché pulp (see page 12)
white glue
white primer
gold liquid leaf paint
acrylic paints: white, yellow,
  ocher, turquoise and
  brown
sealing spray
gloss varnish

EQUIPMENT
bowl, for molding
scissors
large, medium and fine
  paintbrushes
pair of compasses
pencil
paper tissue
paint-mixing container

1 Apply a coat of petroleum jelly to the inside of the bowl. Line it with strips of wet newspaper. Put the papier-mâché pulp into the bowl in an even layer about ½ in deep. Allow to dry in a warm, dry place for about five days. Release the bowl from the mold. Cut strips of newspaper, and dip them in white glue. Cover the bowl with the strips.

2 Give the bowl two coats of white primer. Use a pair of compasses to help center the flower motif. Draw out the flower shape freehand.

3 Paint the rim with gold liquid leaf. Decorate the bowl with the acrylic paints. Mix white into all the colors to lighten them and, before the paint dries, dab some off with a paper tissue so that the primer shows through in places. Allow to dry. Spray with sealing spray. Finally, give the bowl a coat of varnish.

MIRRORED SUNFLOWER BOX

This elaborately detailed and decorated mirror box is reminiscent of South-American art. The mirror is hidden behind painted doors, which can be closed when not in use.

YOU WILL NEED

MATERIALS
corrugated cardboard
newspaper
white glue
masking tape
white primer
gouache paints: red, blue,
  orange, yellow and white
gloss varnish
gold liquid leaf paint
mirror
epoxy glue
2 small brass-door hinges

EQUIPMENT
craft knife
self-healing cutting mat
ruler
pencil
paint-mixing container
fine paintbrushes

1 Cut out all the box pieces from corrugated cardboard. The arch-shaped back is 10 in high and 5 in wide at the base. The sides are 1½ in deep. Create a recess 1½ in deep and 3 in square, for the mirror to sit in. Cut a 5 in flat square frame for the outside of the recess. Cut a 2¾ in square piece of cardboard in half for the doors. Cut out the petals to be attached around the sides of the box. Cut out the sunflowers and the stems, bulking out the middles by gluing on scrunched-up newspaper. Assemble the box, using masking tape. Leave off the doors.

2 Cover with several layers of newspaper soaked in diluted white glue. Allow to dry. Paint with white primer, and allow to dry.

3 Paint all the pieces. When dry, apply several coats of varnish. Add details in gold. Glue on the mirror. Pierce three holes in the shelf, and glue in the sunflowers. Glue the hinges and doors in position.

SUNFLOWER MIRROR

You may not always feel cheerful when you look in the mirror, but this sunflower face is sure to lift your spirits. It could grace a dresser or look good as a decorative object in any room in the house.

YOU WILL NEED

MATERIALS
cardboard
modeling clay
small terracotta or plastic
  flowerpot
plaster of Paris
8 in of 8 mm diameter
  aluminum tubing
2¾ in diameter round mirror
acrylic paints: yellow, white,
  chocolate-brown and green

EQUIPMENT
pair of compasses
pencil
ruler
scissors
rolling pin
modeling tools
plaster-mixing container
old ballpoint pen
paint-mixing container
medium paintbrush

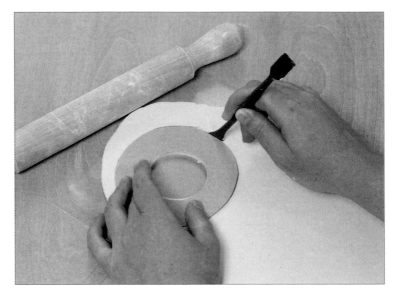

1 Cut out a circular cardboard template of 4¾ in diameter. Cut out a 2½ in diameter circle from the center. Roll out a sheet of clay to ¼ in thick, and use the template to cut out two rings.

2 Seal the drainage holes in the bottom of the flowerpot with clay. Mix up the plaster, and pour it into the pot. When the plaster is semi-dry, insert the tube in the middle and allow to dry completely. Remove the tube. Place the mirror in the center of one ring, and place the tube with one end resting on the bottom edge of the circle. Put the second ring on top. Then seal the edges together with a wet modeling tool.

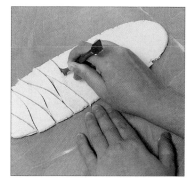

3 Roll out another sheet of clay ⅛ in thick, in a long, oval shape. Cut out regular flower-petal shapes.

4 Attach petals all around the back of the mirror, sealing the edges with the tool. Then attach petals to the front, so they cover the spaces between the back petals. Bend some of the petals to make the sunflower more realistic.

5 Roll two long, thin "sausages" of clay, and flatten them. Put one on top of the joint between the petals and the mirror and one at the edge of the mirror. Press an old pen into the "sausages" to create little depressions all over.

6 Mix the two yellow and white paints to make a sunny yellow. Paint the sunflower petals yellow.

7 Paint the border around the mirror with chocolate-brown. Remove the tube, and paint it green. Reinsert the tube in the flowerpot. Fit the mirror on top.

PLATTER WITH PAINTED SUNFLOWERS

Vibrant, hand-painted flowerheads give an exuberant decorative finish to a plain terracotta flowerpot base. You could use the same idea to decorate a matching flowerpot for a stunningly floral container display. Ceramic flowerpots and bases come in many different sizes, and they are ideal for painting on. Use ceramic paints, for a translucent quality, or acrylics, for a brighter, bolder look.

YOU WILL NEED

MATERIALS
ceramic flowerpot base
white primer
acrylic paints: red, yellow,
  brown and green
matte varnish

EQUIPMENT
medium and fine paintbrushes
pencil
paint-mixing container

1 Apply primer to the flowerpot base. Sketch out your pattern, freehand, in pencil. Fill in the background in red acrylic paint. Fill in the flowers in yellow.

2 Use a fine brush to draw the outlines for the detail in the central flower.

3 With the fine brush, fill in the detail in the central and other flowers, in brown and green. When dry, give the whole platter two or three coats of varnish, allowing to dry between coats.

SUNFLOWER BADGE

This cheerful sunflower face can be worn as a badge or brooch and would enhance a plain sweater or jacket. The colors are very bright and would go equally well with black or neutral-colored clothes.

YOU WILL NEED

MATERIALS
¼ in thick birch-veneer plywood
wood glue
white primer
acrylic paints: yellow, red,
 chocolate-brown and gold
gloss varnish
brooch pin

EQUIPMENT
pencil
pair of compasses
coping saw or fretsaw
medium- and fine-grade
 sandpaper
medium and fine paintbrushes
paint-mixing container

1 Draw a circle for the flower-center on the plywood with the compasses. Draw the petals, freehand, around the center. Draw another circle the same size as the center. Cut out these two shapes with a saw.

2 Sand any rough edges on the flower. Sand the circle's edge to a curve. Glue the circle to the center of the flower shape, with wood glue. Paint with white primer, and allow to dry. Sand lightly.

3 Paint in the flower details with the acrylic paints. Mix yellow and red to make a golden-yellow for the petals. Paint the center brown. When dry, add gold dots to the center. Apply a coat of gloss varnish. When the varnish is dry, stick the brooch pin on the back of the badge with wood glue.

SUNFLOWER HOOK BOARD

This is both useful and attractive. Mount it on the wall near the door so spare keys are always on hand and easily found. This mottled blue-and-gray background sets off the bright colors of the flower well, but you could adapt the colors to match your own kitchen-color scheme.

YOU WILL NEED

MATERIALS
½ in thick pine board
white primer
acrylic paints: blue, gray, white, red, yellow and green
3 brass hooks

EQUIPMENT
pencil
ruler
pair of compasses
coping saw or fretsaw
medium- and fine-grade sandpaper
medium, small and fine paintbrushes
paint-mixing container
drill, with number 10 bit

1 Mark out the shape of the board on the wood. It is 3¾ in wide, 4 in high to the shoulder and 5 in high to the top of the curve. Use compasses to draw in the curved top.

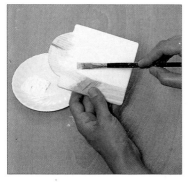

2 Cut out the board, and sand any rough edges. Paint with primer. When dry, sand lightly. Paint the board with the base color, using a mixture of blue, gray and white to give a mottled effect.

3 When the base is dry, sketch in your flower shape, freehand, in pencil. Paint the flower white. Color in the flower, mixing colors, as necessary. Paint the stem green. When the paint is dry, sand it lightly with fine sandpaper to give a "distressed" finish. Drill a hole in the top center of the board. Screw in the brass hooks along the bottom.

HAND-PAINTED FLORAL TILES

This is a great idea for decorating plain ceramic tiles, which could then be framed and hung on the wall as a change from prints and paintings. Ceramic paints give a translucent quality to the color, which enhances the glazed surface.

YOU WILL NEED

MATERIALS
plain white glazed tiles
masking tape
ceramic paints: green, yellow, red and blue

EQUIPMENT
scissors
medium and fine paintbrushes
paint-mixing container

1 Wash the tiles in hot, soapy water. Allow to dry. Trace the motif from the template at the back of the book, and enlarge it if necessary. Turn the paper over, and rub over the main flower outline with a soft pencil. Tape the transfer to the tile. Draw over the outline with a hard pencil to transfer the motif onto the tile.

2 Using a medium brush and thin layers of paint, color in the leaves and petals. Then bake the tile in the oven to set the paint according to the manufacturer's instructions.

3 With a fine brush and blue paint, draw in the outline and detail of the petals, leaves and stalk. Paint tiny dots in the center of the flower. Transfer the four corner motifs in the same way, and with a fine brush, paint them blue. Set the paint by baking the tile again. The tile will withstand gentle cleaning, but not a dishwasher.

SUNFLOWER STORAGE CANISTER

Transform plain, metal storage canisters quickly by spraying them with aerosol paint and then painting cheerful sunflowers all over them. This is an inexpensive alternative to the painted storage jars on sale in houseware stores. A matching set of six or so would really look cheerful all together on a kitchen shelf.

YOU WILL NEED

MATERIALS
plain, metal storage canister
matte blue spray paint
acrylic paints: yellow, orange,
  brown and cream
acrylic sealer spray

EQUIPMENT
paint-mixing container
medium and fine paintbrushes

1 Wash the canister to remove any grease. Dry thoroughly. Spray the can and lid with the blue paint, building the color up with several fine layers and allowing each one to dry before applying the next. This will prevent the paint from running.

2 Using the acrylic paints, paint in the sunflowers. For each one, paint a yellow circle about 1¼ in in diameter, and then evenly space the petals around the edge. Repeat the motif, placing it evenly around the canister until the whole surface is covered. Allow to dry, and then apply another layer of paint.

3 Add more color to the yellow petals to give a feeling of depth. Paint the centers brown. Paint in the seeds with circles of brown paint, highlighting with cream. When the paint is dry, spray the canister and lid with an acrylic sealer to protect the surface. The canister will withstand gentle cleaning, but not a dishwasher.

SUNFLOWER MAGNET

This refrigerator magnet in the shape of a sunflower will brighten up the kitchen on the darkest of mornings. It's extremely easy and quick to make. You could consider making a whole row of them as a reminder, in the middle of winter, of the pleasures of the garden.

YOU WILL NEED

MATERIALS
¼ in thick birch-veneer plywood
wood glue
white primer
acrylic paints: yellow, red,
  green, chocolate-brown and
  gold
gloss varnish
small magnet
epoxy glue

EQUIPMENT
pencil
pair of compasses
coping saw or fretsaw
medium- and fine-grade
  sandpaper
medium and fine paintbrushes
paint-mixing container

1 With compasses, draw a circle on the plywood for the center of the flower. Draw in the petals, leaf and stem freehand. Draw another circle the same size on the plywood. Cut these shapes out with a saw.

2 Sand any rough edges off the flower shape. Sand the circle's edge to a curve. Then glue the circle to the center of the flower with wood glue.

3 Paint with primer. Allow to dry, and then sand lightly. Paint in the flower details with acrylic paints. Mix a golden-yellow, and paint the petals. Paint the stem and leaves green. Paint the center brown. When dry, add darker detail on the petals, veining on the leaves and gold dots on the center. When dry, apply a coat of varnish. When the varnish is dry, stick the magnet on the back of the flower with epoxy glue.

GILDED SUNFLOWER CANDLESTICK

Candlelight gives a magical glow to a room, and this shimmering, gilded candlestick will really heighten the atmosphere. Both silver and gold are used here in a dramatic effect. The sunflower motif is a relief design built up with layers of gesso, and the depth of the relief enhances the light and shade effect.

YOU WILL NEED

MATERIALS
turned-wood candlestick
red-oxide primer
3-hour oil size
aluminum leaf transfer book
acrylic gesso
Dutch gold leaf transfer book
black watercolor paint
methylated alcohol-based
  varnish

EQUIPMENT
medium and fine paintbrushes
large stencil brush
paint-mixing container
rag

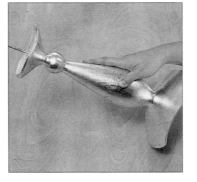

1 Prime the candlestick all over with red-oxide and allow to dry. Then paint it with size. Allow to dry for three hours. When the size is "squeaky" it is ready for gilding. Begin gilding the candlestick with aluminum leaf, rubbing it with a dry stencil brush, so it adheres to the size. Repeat until covered.

2 Paint a fine layer of acrylic gesso, freehand, in a sunflower shape. Allow to dry. Build up the relief with three or four layers of gesso.

3 Paint lines of gesso in the center to make a lattice pattern. Allow to dry.

4 Paint the sunflower with red-oxide primer to seal the surface and to act as a base coat for the gilding. Allow to dry.

5 Paint the sunflower with size, and allow to dry.

6 Once the size is "squeaky", lay a sheet of Dutch gold leaf on the flower.

7 Rub it with the stencil brush, using the bristles to push the metal into the grooves, so it adheres.

8 Put a little black water-color on a rag, and rub it into the lattice to darken it, giving an effect of greater depth. Finally, give the whole candlestick a coat of varnish.

SUNFLOWER MOSAIC

S hards of china and mirror wink in the sun, on this attractive and unusual wall decoration. Collect bright fragments of china in a harmonious blend of colors for your design.

MATERIALS
¼ in thick plywood
electric cable
masking tape
white glue
white primer
china fragments
mirror strips
tile adhesive
grout
cement dye

EQUIPMENT
pencil
coping saw or fretsaw
medium- and fine-grade
 sandpaper
awl
wire cutters
paintbrush
tile nippers
rubber gloves
dust mask
grout-mixing container
nail brush
soft cloth

1 Draw out the sunflower on the plywood. Cut it out with a saw, and sand any rough edges. Make two holes with an awl. Strip the cable, and cut a short length of wire. Push the ends of the wire through the holes from the back. Fix the ends with masking tape at the front. Seal the front with some diluted white glue and the back with primer.

2 Cut the china and mirror strips into irregular shapes, using the tile nippers. Stick them to the plywood, using tile adhesive. Dip each fragment in the adhesive, and scoop up enough to cover the sticking surface. The adhesive should squelch out around the edge of the mosaic to make sure it adheres securely. Allow to dry thoroughly overnight.

3 Wearing rubber gloves and a dust mask, mix up the grout with cement dye, as directed by the manufacturer. Press a small amount of wet grout into the gaps. Allow to dry for about five minutes. Brush off any excess with a nail brush. Leave again for five minutes, and then polish with a clean, soft cloth. Allow to dry thoroughly overnight.

GILDED SUNFLOWER LAMP

A silver gilded lamp base and a golden shade form a light source that will be a glowing focal point in any room. When lit, the gilded lamp seems to shimmer. The effect in a dark corner is magical.

YOU WILL NEED

MATERIALS
turned-wood lamp base
red-oxide primer
3-hour oil size
aluminum leaf transfer book
18 in parchment shade
white glue
Dutch gold leaf transfer book
black watercolor paint
methylated alcohol-based
  varnish

EQUIPMENT
medium and fine paintbrushes
large stencil brush
white carboard
craft knife
pencil
self-healing cutting mat
cotton wool

1 Use red-oxide to prime the lamp base. Allow to dry. Then paint the lamp base with size, and allow to dry for three hours. When the size is "squeaky", it is ready for gilding. Lay the aluminum leaf on the base. Rub it with the stencil brush so it adheres to the base. Repeat until the base is covered.

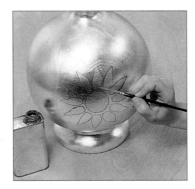

2 Draw the sunflower, freehand, onto white cardboard. Carefully cut out the stencil from the cardbaord with a craft knife. Trace the outline onto the base, through the stencil, with a sharp pencil.

3 Paint the size onto the stenciled sunflower shapes, and allow it to dry for three hours, until "squeaky".

4 Meanwhile, paint a small area of the lampshade with slightly diluted white glue. Immediately lay a sheet of Dutch gold on top and rub with the stencil brush, so it adheres. Quickly brush off any excess, so the effect is slightly patchy.

5 Repeat with another small area, applying Dutch gold as before.

6 Continue until the lamp-shade is covered. Seal the lampshade with another coat of diluted white glue.

7 When the size on the base is "squeaky", cover the design with a sheet of Dutch gold. Rub it gently with the stencil brush, so that the gold adheres to the size. Brush off any excess.

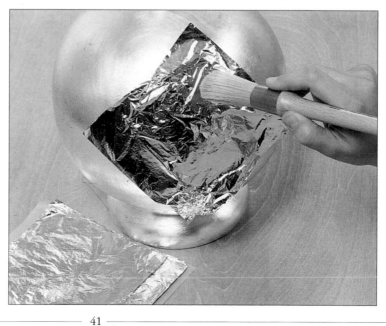

8 Put a little watercolor paint on a piece of cotton wool, and rub it into the center of the sunflower to give a mottled or stippled effect. Finally, give the whole base a coat of varnish.

WIRE SUNFLOWER MOBILE

This mobile has a light and airy feeling. Wire can be bent into a variety of interesting and attractive shapes with pliers, and these sunflowers have the pleasing simplicity of a child's drawing. This would make a lovely decoration for a child's room or for any sunny corner.

YOU WILL NEED

MATERIALS
2 mm, 1.6 mm and 1 mm thick aluminum wire
binding wire
white primer aerosol car paint
aerosol car paints: yellow, brown and green
masking tape
strong green thread
strong clear glue

EQUIPMENT
wire cutters
long ruler
3 round containers (about 2½ in, 2 in and 1 in diameter)
indelible marker pen
flat-nosed pliers
snub-nosed pliers
scrap paper
scissors

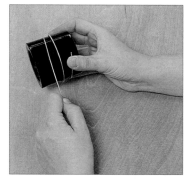

1 Cut lengths of wire for the struts and flowers with wire cutters, as follows: large strut: 23½ in of 2 mm wire; short struts: 15 in of 2 mm wire; small ring: ¾ in of 2 mm wire; large flower: 42 in of 1.6 mm wire; center circle of large flower: 2¾ in of 2 mm wire; medium-size flowers with stems: 2 x 57 in of 1.6 mm wire; center circles of medium flowers: 2 x 2¼ in of 2 mm wire; small flowers: 5 x 16½ in of 1 mm wire; center circles of small flowers: 5 x 1¼ in of 1.6 mm wire. Bend the wires for the centers of all the flowers around circular containers that are slightly smaller than the outside diameters of the centers.

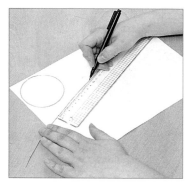

2 For the large flower, mark along the wire with the marker pen ¾ in from one end and then at ten intervals of 4 in.

3 Bend the wire into folds at every mark.

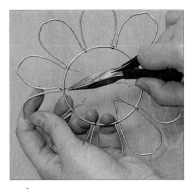

4 Pinch each of the folds together tightly with the flat-nosed pliers.

5 Using snub-nosed pliers, bend the center peaks and curve the petals into shape. Snip off the ends, leaving a small hook for binding the flower to its center.

6 Bind in the center circle with binding wire, folding the binding wire over each loop and twisting it tightly to secure it. Repeat the process for the small flowers, marking the wire at ½ in from the end and at ten intervals of 1½ in.

7 For the medium-size flowers with stems, mark 13¾ in from the end and at ten intervals of 3 in apart, leaving another 14 in end. Fold the petals as for the large flower. Use all of the remaining wire for the leaves.

8 Bind the two stem wires together, using binding wire, to secure the leaves at the base. Bind the center circle as in step 6. Bend the wires for the struts, using the templates at the back of the book as a guide. Spray everything with white primer. Allow to dry. Spray the pieces in the appropriate colors, masking off any areas as necessary, and allowing to dry between colors. Make up the mobile, securing the threads to the pieces with a knot and a little glue.

FLOWER-STENCILED WRAPPING PAPER

I f you have taken trouble to find a really special gift, homemade wrapping paper is the perfect finishing touch. Once the stencil is cut, this design doesn't take long to do, and its effect is magnificent. You could use the stencil again and again, changing the paint and paper colors as you wish. It would be most suited for wrapping large items, to maximize the impact of the sunflowers.

YOU WILL NEED

MATERIALS
green crêpe paper
acrylic or stencil paints:
  raw umber, white and yellow

EQUIPMENT
pencil
acetate sheet
craft knife
self-healing cutting mat
paint-mixing container
stencil brush

1 Trace the templates from the back of the book, and enlarge them if necessary. Transfer them to the acetate sheet. The design is made from two pieces, the petals and the center. Use a craft knife to cut each part out separately.

2 Using the flower-center stencil, apply raw umber paint to the crêpe paper. Position the stencil at random, covering the paper. Be sure to allow enough room between the centers for the petals.

3 Lighten the raw umber with white paint, and apply as a highlight.

4 Take the second stencil and, taking care to align it properly over the first, stencil the petals in yellow. Allow to dry.

NEEDLEPOINT SUNFLOWER CUSHION

This cushion would be perfect for an easy chair in the kitchen. The cushion is worked in simple stitches, but they produce a really stylish effect.

YOU WILL NEED

MATERIALS
10 in square, 12-count, single-thread canvas
masking tape
2 skeins each 3-strand yarn in dark brown, 2 shades of mid-blue and light cream
1 skein each 3-strand yarn in: light brown, light yellow, dark yellow and warm, light brown
7½ in square velvet
polyester batting
matching thread

EQUIPMENT
tracing paper
pencil
scissors
felt-tipped pens
ruler
tapestry needle
straight pins
sewing needle
drawing pins

1 Bind the edges of the canvas with masking tape. Trace the template from the back of the book, and enlarge it if necessary. Place the canvas over the tracing. Trace the main outline onto the center of the canvas, and then fill in the detailed lines. All the stitches are sewn with two strands of yarn.

2 Work the main outline in dark brown tent stitch. Then fill in the petals with tent stitch, and the flower-center with upright cross stitch. Rule a 6½ in square around the flower, and fill in the background with cushion stitch. Work with two different strands of blue wool together, and alternate blue and cream squares.

3 Block the canvas by spraying it lightly with water. Stretch and pin it squarely. When dry, trim the canvas to leave ½ in all around the edge. Pin velvet to the backing, with right sides together. Stitch around three sides and turn right sides out. Insert the batting and slip stitch the gap.

SUNFLOWER SILK CUSHION COVER

A spectacular sunflower head makes a really bold statement on this cushion cover. This would look wonderful in a light, bright, modern design scheme. The drama of the overall conception is balanced by the delicacy of the hand painted effect.

YOU WILL NEED

MATERIALS
white silk-satin 2½ times the size of the cushion pad, plus a ⅝ in seam allowance
silk paints: yellow, red, blue, turquoise and ultramarine
matching silk thread
cushion pad

EQUIPMENT
fine-art stretchers or large frame
double-sided tape
vanishing fabric marker or tailor's chalk
paint-mixing container
large flat-bristled, medium and fine paintbrushes
sewing machine
pins
needle

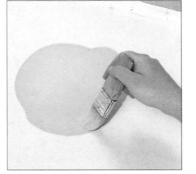

1 Place double-sided tape all around the stretchers or frame. Fold the silk-satin into three panels, two the size of the pad and one half the size (to form the flap). Mark the panels with marker or chalk. Stretch the silk on the frame so that the front (the middle panel) is centered on the frame. Brush yellow paint from the center outward, using the flat brush.

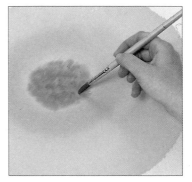

2 Immediately, before the paint dries, add red paint to the yellow to make orange, and redefine the center part of the circle. Immediately add blue to the paint to make a green, and make a smaller circle in the center of the orange. Add dots in the center with more blue. Allow to dry.

3 Define the petals with red. Fill in the background with shades of blue. Turn under, and stitch a narrow double hem on each short edge. Fold the silk back into its original panels with right sides facing, so that the flap covers half the front. Fold the back over both, and pin and stitch the side seams. Turn the cover right side out. Insert the cushion pad, and slip stitch the gap.

SUNFLOWER-STENCILED PEG-BAG

This peg-bag is made from practical, unbleached calico. The sunflowers are worked in dry stencil fabric paint. Once set, the stencils will be hand-washable.

YOU WILL NEED

MATERIALS
20 x 30 in unbleached calico
12 in child's wooden coat hanger
yellow and brown dry stencil
 fabric paints
matching thread
1 yd yellow ribbon

EQUIPMENT
tracing paper
soft and hard pencils
stencil cardboard
self-healing cutting mat
craft knife
dressmaker's scissors
pins
vanishing fabric marker
2 stencil brushes
iron
sewing machine
needle

1 Trace the stencil template from the back of the book, and enlarge it if necessary. Transfer the outline on to the stencil cardboard. Cut out the stencil with a craft knife. From the unbleached calico, cut out two 14 x 14 in squares.

2 Pin the squares together, place the hanger along one edge, and draw around it with the marker. Cut this curve. Stencil a sunflower in each corner of one piece of fabric. Allow the paint to dry, and set it according to the manufacturer's instructions.

3 Cut a 4 x 10 in calico facing for the front opening. Baste the facing on to the center top of the stenciled fabric. Sew two 8 in lines of straight stitch, ¼ in away from both sides of the center. Cut in between these lines, and turn the facing to the wrong side. Press and top stitch around the opening. With right sides together, stitch the back to the front. Turn right sides out, fit the coat hanger in place, and finish off with a yellow bow.

APPLIQUED SUNFLOWERS GREETING CARD

A homemade card is much nicer than a bought one, and this cheery sunflower design, worked in a combination of appliqué and embroidery, would be perfect for someone with a high-summer birthday. A sunflower card would be a wonderful complement to the stenciled sunflower wrapping paper.

YOU WILL NEED

MATERIALS
yellow and brown fabric scraps
background fabric
fabric glue
embroidery thread
green paper scraps
card paper and envelope
paper glue

EQUIPMENT
tracing paper
pencil
paper
scissors
needle

1 Trace the template from the back of the book and enlarge it, if necessary. Transfer the outline to the yellow fabric, and cut it out. Then cut out the smaller centers from brown.

3 On the dark brown ring, sew from the outer to the inner edge in one large stitch, like a very loose, random satin stitch to give a textured effect. Continue all the way around.

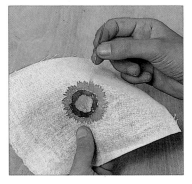

2 Stick the yellow piece onto the base fabric and the brown one on top. Then stick the third piece on top. Sew from the edge of the inner ring, using a running stitch on the center piece.

4 On the center piece, sew running stitches at random, to give the effect of seeds. Sew on the green paper leaves. Check for any loose threads on the back, and tie them in. Trim the fabric to the correct size for the aperture of the card. Stick the appliqué in position cleanly.

CHILD'S APPLIQUED T-SHIRT

An ordinary T-shirt is transformed, with appliquéd fabric scraps, machine embroidery and beads, into something really special. There's no reason why the same idea couldn't be used for an adult-size T-shirt, as well.

YOU WILL NEED

MATERIALS
*12 in square iron-on
  fusible bonding web
yellow, orange and brown
  cotton fabric scraps
unbleached cotton T-shirt
light orange and brown thread
small orange beads*

EQUIPMENT
*pencil
dressmaker's scissors
iron
pressing cloth
sewing machine*

1 Trace the template from the back of the book, and enlarge it to fit the T-shirt. Number the petals consecutively 1–12. Trace the even-numbered petals onto the paper side of the bonding. Cut them out. Attach the bonding to the yellow cotton, using a cool iron. Repeat with the other petals and the orange fabric and then with the brown cotton for the center.

2 Cut out all the shapes around the outlines, and remove the backing paper. Place the petals in a circle on the front of the T-shirt, using the template as a guide. Iron them in place, using a cool iron and a pressing cloth.

3 Thread the sewing machine with orange thread, and set it to a closely spaced medium-size zigzag. Stitch around the edges of all the petals to conceal the raw edges. Iron the flower-center in position, and sew around its circumference with brown thread. Using brown thread, sew the beads onto the flower-center, evenly scattered.

TEMPLATES

If the templates need to be enlarged, either use a grid system or a photocopier. For the grid system, trace the template, and draw a grid of evenly-spaced squares over your tracing. To scale up, draw a larger grid onto another piece of paper. Copy the outline onto the second grid by taking each square individually and drawing the relevant part of the outline in the larger square. For tracing templates, you will need tracing paper, a pencil, cardboard or paper and scissors.

Hand-painted Floral Tile, p28

Sunflower-stenciled Peg-bag, p54

Child's Appliquéd T-shirt, p58

Appliquéd Sunflowers Greeting Card, p56

Wire Sunflower Mobile, p44

Flower-stenciled Wrapping Paper, p48

Needlepoint Sunflower Cushion, p50

ACKNOWLEDGEMENTS

The author and publishers would like to thank the following people for designing the projects in this book:

Ofer Acoo

Sunflower Mirror pp18–21; Sunflower Silk Cushion Cover pp52–53

Madeleine Adams

Gold-rimmed Sunflower Bowl pp14–15

Lilli Curtiss

Gilded Sunflower Candlestick pp34–37; Gilded Sunflower Lamp pp40–43

Lucinda Ganderton

Hand-painted Floral Tiles pp28–29; Sunflower Storage Canister pp30–31; Needlepoint Sunflower Cushion pp50–51; Sunflower-stenciled Peg-bag pp54–55; Child's Appliquéd T-shirt pp58–59

Jill Hancock

Sunflower Badge pp24–25; Sunflower Hook Board pp26–27; Sunflower Magnet pp32–33

Izzy Moreau

Papier-mâché Pitcher with Sunflower pp12–13; Platter with Painted Sunflowers pp22–23

Cleo Mussie

Sunflower Mosaic pp38–39

Kim Rowley

Mirrored Sunflower Box pp16–17

Kellie-Marie Townsend

Appliquéd Sunflowers Greeting Card pp56–57

Josephine Whitfield

Sunflower-stenciled Wrapping Paper pp48–49